THE QUARTER HORSE

by Gail B. Stewart

Illustrated with photographs
by William Muñoz

Reading consultant:

John Manning, Professor of Reading
University of Minnesota

Capstone Press

M I N N E A P O L I S

Printed in the United States of America.

Capstone Press • 2440 Fernbrook Lane • Minneapolis, MN 55447

Editorial Director   John Coughlan
Managing Editor   John Martin
Copy Editor   Gil Chandler

Library of Congress Cataloging-in-Publication Data

Stewart, Gail, 1949-
  The quarter horse / by Gail Stewart ; photographs by William Muñoz.
    p. cm.
  Includes bibliographical references and index.
  ISBN 1-56065-242-X
  1. Quarter horse--Juvenile literature. [1. Quarter horse.
2. Horses.] I. Muñoz, William, ill. II. Title.
SF293.Q3S74   1995
636.1'33--dc20   94-26763
                                                      CIP
                                                            AC

ISBN: 1-56065-242-X

99 98 97 96 95   8 7 6 5 4 3 2 1

Table of Contents

Quick Facts about the Quarter Horse

Description

Height:
14.2 to 15.2 **hands** (equal to four-inch [ten-centimeter] segments) from the ground to the top of the shoulders. That works out to between 57 and 61 inches (142 and 152 centimeters) tall.

Weight:
1,050 to 1,250 lbs. (476 to 567 kilograms).

Physical features:
powerful muscles, especially in rump and back legs; small ears; large eyes; short, wide back; deep, sloping shoulders.

Colors:
13 solid colors including gray, black, white, **chestnut**, palomino, and pinto.

Development

Ancestor breeds:
Thoroughbred horses and Spanish **jennets**.

Place of origin:
North America.

Current habitat:
over 3 million are registered in the United States and in 64 countries around the world.

Food

Hay, grasses such as **timothy** and **clover**, grain (especially oats and **bran**), and plenty of water. Every day a Quarter Horse needs about 14 pounds (6 kilograms) of hay and grasses, between 4 and 12 quarts (3.8 and 11.3 liters) of oats and bran, and 12 gallons (45.5 liters) of water.

Life History

Life span: a well-cared-for Quarter Horse may live from 20 to 30 years.

Reproductive life: stallions are bred when they are about two years old; mares when they are three or four. Quarter Horse mares carry their **foals** for 11 months before giving birth.

Uses

Quarter Horses are used to herd and tend cattle in the United States and Canada. On farms they are sometimes harnessed in teams and used to pull wagons.

Chapter 1

The "Do-It-All" Horse

Every kind of horse is suited to something. Some have long legs to carry them quickly along a racetrack. Strong and sturdy horses can pull heavy loads. Horses with a gentle nature are suitable for pleasure riding.

There is one kind of horse, however, that is suited to almost anything. It is the Quarter Horse, called the "do-it-all" horse by many people. A Quarter Horse can race, play polo, jump, and help a cowboy tend cattle.

Few animals can do so many things so well. What other horse can outrun a motorcycle in a quarter-mile (.4 kilometer) race? What other horse can go eye-to-eye with a fierce Texas steer, or turn sharply at full gallop?

With such talents, it is no wonder that the Quarter Horse is the most popular breed in the world. There are more than 3 million Quarter Horses registered today. Quarter Horses can be found in all 50 states and in 64 other countries around the world.

Where did Quarter Horses come from? How are Quarter Horses different from other breeds? And why is this breed so good at so many different things?

Chapter 2

The Beginnings of the Quarter Horse

The Quarter Horse is the result of breeding two different types of horses–the Spanish **jennet** and the English **Thoroughbred horse**.

Spanish Horses

When Spanish explorers sailed to the New World in the 16th century, they took horses with them. The Spaniards knew there were no horses in what is now America.

These Spanish horses were known as jennets. They were stocky, muscular, and shorter than many other breeds. Although they were not long-legged racers like some other European horses, jennets were quick and intelligent. They were easy to train, too, and very dependable.

The Spanish horses thrived in the New World. Within a few years, the small number of jennets grew. Some ran free and wild. These later became known as **mustangs**.

Other jennets were kept by the Spanish settlers and used to herd cattle on large ranches in Mexico. Some were traded to Native American tribes, who trained the horses to help in hunting. It was much easier to hunt buffalo and other game from the back of a quick, strong horse!

English Horses Come to America

In the early 17th century, English settlers came to North America. They built colonies along the east coast. Like the Spanish, the English colonists brought horses from home.

The English horses, called Thoroughbreds, were quite different from the Spanish jennets. They were not as muscular or as stocky as the Spanish horses. Thoroughbreds were tall and sleek, with long legs.

Life in the colonies was difficult, and animals had to do as much work as their owners did. Thoroughbred horses were used for pulling plows and hauling heavy loads. Sometimes they were hitched to wagons. The colonists also saddled them up for long rides.

A New Breed

It was not long before the English colonists began to breed their Thoroughbreds with Spanish horses. The offspring inherited the best parts of both parents. They were taller than the Spanish horses but shorter than Thoroughbreds. They were muscular and strong, especially in their hindquarters. Their most exciting quality, however, was their speed.

The Fastest Horse in the Quarter-Mile

The colonists were used to fast horses. In England, Thoroughbred racing was very popular. Nothing was as thrilling as watching a pack of sleek, long-legged Thoroughbred horses run head to head, nose to nose.

Although there were no race tracks in the colonies, the settlers often organized short races through the streets of their towns. The distance was usually a quarter of a mile (.4 kilometer). At that length, people could see the whole race from start to finish.

The powerful muscles in the new horse's rump and legs gave it a fast start. With three or four steps it reached top speed. A taller horse might win a long race, but it took more time to get its long legs moving. The smaller horse usually won the quarter-mile, much to everyone's surprise.

The colonists named this new, swift breed the "quarter-of-a-mile running horse." The name was later shortened to Quarter Horse.

Chapter 3

The Development of the Quarter Horse

For a while, it seemed that everyone wanted a Quarter Horse. By the 1800s, however, there was less demand for Quarter Horses.

As America grew, there was a change in the kind of horse racing people enjoyed. Spectators grew tired of quarter-mile races that were over in less than 30 seconds. To make the races longer, oval tracks like those in Europe were built. The longer oval tracks gave the

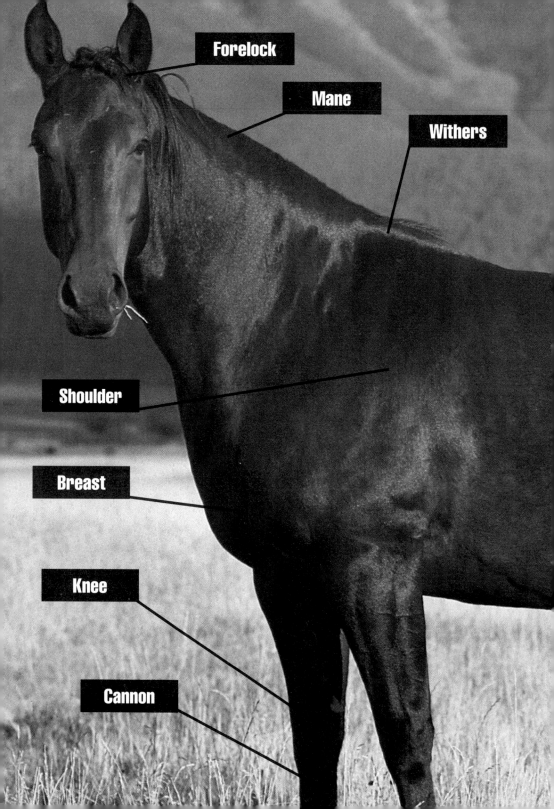

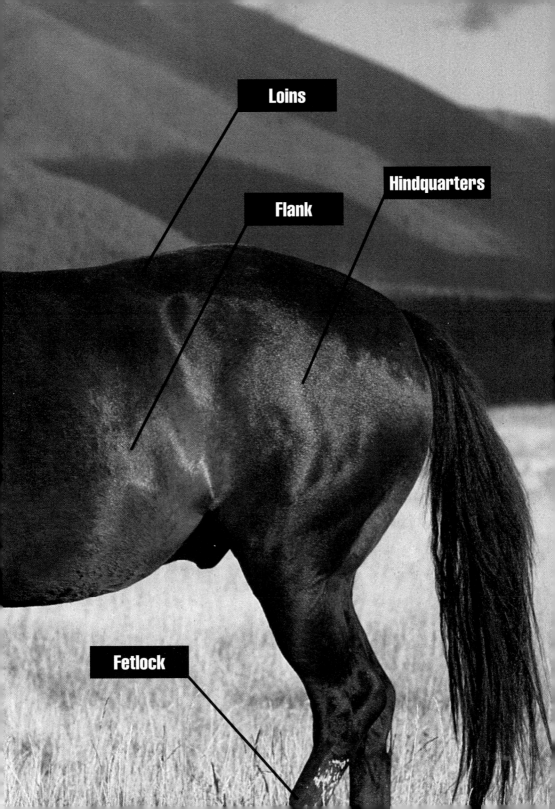

Loins

Flank

Hindquarters

Fetlock

advantage to tall horses. The little Quarter
Horse was no longer in demand as a racer.

Moving West

There was one group of Americans who still
needed the Quarter Horse. They were the
pioneers and settlers moving west. The strong
Quarter Horse could help a pioneer plow fields
and clear trees for pasture. It could haul logs,
remove stumps, and pull heavy wagons.

No job was better suited to the Quarter
Horse than that of herding cattle. After 1860,
huge herds of cattle were moved north each
year from Texas to railroad lines in Kansas.
From there, the cattle were shipped to cities in
the East, where people wanted beef. The
cowboys who led the great cattle drives needed
good horses.

Cow Ponies

Quarter Horses quickly became the hard-
working partners of the cowboys, who called
these horses "cow ponies." The Quarter Horse
worked well with cattle. Unlike some other

breeds, it was not nervous around cows. When a cowboy rode alongside a stampeding herd or had to rope a cow for branding, his Quarter Horse did not hesitate to carry him wherever he needed to go.

The Quarter Horse could endure many hardships. A cattle drive could take months under tough conditions. Horses might go for days without enough water and with only the toughest prairie grass to graze on. When icy rains or dust storms hit, Quarter Horses would wait patiently without shelter for the signal to begin working again.

The Quarter Horses did their work, and the cowboys admired them for it. As one cowboy wrote in his diary, "I couldn't have done a minute's work without my horse. He is smarter than I am, and has tons more common sense. I figure the trail boss would be more upset if my old horse ran off than if I did!"

Chapter 4

The Quarter Horse Today

Things have changed for the Quarter Horse in the 20th century. Cattle drives no longer take place. Cattle-herding is done with jeeps and even helicopters. Even though Quarter Horses are still used in the West, they are not as important to cowboys and ranchers as they once were.

The American Quarter Horse Association

In 1940 worried owners met to discuss the future of the Quarter Horse. Cow ponies were being replaced by machines throughout the West. What would happen to the thousands of Quarter Horses who were no longer needed?

To protect the breed, horse owners formed the American Quarter Horse Association, or AQHA. The organization has worked hard to establish the Quarter Horse as an important American breed. Its members believe that the Quarter Horse has been too important a part of history to be forgotten.

One task of the AQHA has been to keep records of all Quarter Horses. These records list the **sire**, or father, and the **dam**, or mother, of every registered Quarter Horse. Is a horse descended from a champion? Was his mother or father a great racer? How many of the horse's ancestors were Thoroughbreds? These are things that people who race horses, or who enter them in competitions, want to know. They are questions that can be answered by the official records of the AQHA.

A Typical Quarter Horse

The **bloodline**, or ancestry, of one Quarter Horse may be very different from that of another. According to the AQHA, however, there are certain physical traits which are shared by all the members of this breed.

Quarter Horses are fairly short. All horses are measured in hands–four-inch (10-centimeter) sections. From the withers (the top of the horse's shoulders) to the ground, Quarter Horses measure between 14 hands, 2 inches (14 hands, 5 centimeters) and 15 hands, 2 inches (15 hands, 5 centimeters).

What the Quarter Horse lacks in height, it makes up in muscle. In fact, an easy way to identify a Quarter Horse is by its muscular legs

and rump. The strength in its hindquarters lets
the horse shift its weight quickly when working
with a herd of cattle.

Quarter Horses have a typical shape that is
well-suited to riding. Their short, wide backs
carry the rider's weight so that the horse does
not get tired. Deep, sloping shoulders keep the
saddle in a good position. This helps the rider
stay balanced.

The legs of a Quarter Horse are strong and straight. The lower leg bone, or **cannon**, in both front and rear legs is shorter than that of other breeds.

The Quarter Horse has small ears and large, wide-set eyes. "Of all the horses, the Quarter Horse seems to have the most interesting eyes," says one breeder. "They are kind, gentle eyes–full of trust. Those eyes always give me the impression that the horse understands everything that is going on."

According to the AQHA, there are 13 color varieties of the breed, including spotted, gray, black, or chestnut. The most common color is reddish-brown, known as **sorrel**. About one-third of the Quarter Horses registered today are sorrel.

Chapter 5

The Quarter Horse in Action

In the past, the Quarter Horse worked to clear land, lead cattle drives, and pull wagons. Now that the days of the pioneers and the great cattle drives are over, what do Quarter Horses do?

Most people who own Quarter Horses use them for pleasure riding. There are many people, however, who still expect their horses to work in one way or another.

Working on the Ranch

While fewer horses are needed to herd cattle today, Quarter Horses are still a valuable part of ranch life.

Cows still need to be moved from pasture to pasture. And in the late spring, calves must be separated from the herd and branded. On a large ranch, these are tough jobs.

Calves are nervous about being away from the herd. When they are separated, they try to get back to their mothers. The cowboys need help to "cut," or separate, calves from the herd.

When a calf starts moving back to the herd, the cowboy directs the Quarter Horse to move with it. If the calf moves to the right, the horse moves to the right. As one horse expert writes, "It's like a dance, except that one partner is unwilling."

The cowboy knows that the horse is doing most of the work. The action happens too quickly for the cowboy to give the horse commands. A good Quarter Horse has "**cow sense**"–the ability to control the movements of

the cow. This is why many ranchers prefer the Quarter Horse to jeeps, trucks, or other modern herding methods.

"Just try to use a truck to move into a herd of nervous cows," laughs one Texas rancher. "The cows will be frightened, and may stampede. The truck is loud and the exhaust smells bad. Besides, I never met a jeep or a truck yet that has an ounce of cow sense. Give me a couple of cowboys and good cow ponies any day!"

The Quarter Horse in Competition

Quarter Horses in horse shows, races, and other competitions can win prize money for their owners.

One of the most famous Quarter Horse events is the All-American Futurity, a horse race held each year in Ruidoso Downs, New Mexico. Two-year-old horses run a fast quarter-mile (.4-kilometer) race that lasts less than 20 seconds. More than $2 million in prize money goes to the winners.

Some competitions demand skill as well as speed. Barrel racing is a favorite among spectators. Each team of horse and rider dashes around three barrels set up in a cloverleaf pattern. Speed is important, but a horse that goes too quickly around a barrel might knock it over and earn a penalty.

There are contests in which the best **"cutting horses"** can show off their talents. The riders have two and a half minutes to cut as many calves as they can from a herd. Many of the best cutting horses come from Texas, where they can practice chasing down calves on real ranches!

A Horse for Everybody

The Quarter Horse has come a long way since the colonists bred Thoroughbreds with the little Spanish horses they found in America.

Although the breed declined in the 1800s, it has made a strong comeback. One horse expert thinks that it is the horse's intelligence and gentle manner that has made the breed so popular.

"The Quarter Horse is very special," says another expert on horses. "Whether you are a racer, a cowboy, a competitor in horse shows, or simply someone who likes to ride for pleasure, the Quarter Horse is the horse for you. There has never been a more exciting breed!"

Glossary

bloodline–the ancestors of a horse. A horse's qualities come from its parents and other ancestors.

bran–a food for horses

cannon–the lower leg bone of a horse

chestnut–a dark brown color, common in Quarter Horses

clover–a flowering grass

cow sense–the special ability of a Quarter Horse to control cattle

cutting horse–a horse used to separate a cow from the rest of the herd and to keep it from returning to the herd

dam–the mother of a horse

foal–a baby horse

hands–four-inch (10-centimeter) segments used to measure a horse. Horses all over the world are measured in hands.

jennet–a short, muscular Spanish horse brought to the New World in the 16th century

mustang–wild horses that descended from the Spanish jennets

sire–father of a horse

sorrel–a reddish-brown color. Many Quarter Horses are sorrel.

Thoroughbred–a tall, long-legged horse brought to America by English colonists

timothy–a grass with flower clusters, grown for hay

To Learn More

Brown, Fern G. *Horses and Foals*. New York: Franklin Watts, 1986.

Clutton-Brock, Juliet. *Horse* (Eyewitness Books). New York: Alfred A. Knopf, 1992.

Henry, Marguerite. *All About Horses*. New York: Random House, 1962.

Murdoch, David H. *Cowboy* (Eyewitness Books). New York: Alfred A. Knopf, 1993.

Patent, Dorothy Hinshaw. *Quarter Horses*. New York: Holiday House, 1985.

Self, Margaret Cabell. *The Complete Book of Horses and Ponies*. New York: McGraw-Hill, 1963.

You can read articles about Quarter Horses in these magazines: *The Quarter Horse Journal, Horse Illustrated,* and *Horse and Rider.*

Some Useful Addresses

American Quarter Horse Association (AQHA) and **American Quarter Horse Heritage Center and Museum**
2601 I-40 East
Amarillo, TX 79104

National Cutting Horse Association
P.O. Box 12155
Fort Worth, TX 76121

Canadian Quarter Horse Association
#360-800-6 Avenue SW
Calgary, AB T2P 3G3

National Cowboy Hall of Fame and Rodeo Hall of Fame
1700 NE 63rd Street
Oklahoma City, OK 73111

Canadian Professional Rodeo Association
2116-27th Ave. N.E.
Calgary, AB T2E 7A6

Index